The Snowman™

SUITE FOR VIOLIN & PIANO

Arranged by David Mather

Music-Box Dance

Walking in the Air

Dance of the Snowmen

CHESTER MUSIC
part of *The Music Sales* *Group*
London / New York / Paris / Sydney / Copenhagen / Berlin / Madrid / Hong Kong / Tokyo

Published by
CHESTER MUSIC LIMITED
14-15 Berners Street, London W1T 3LJ, UK.

Exclusive Distributors:
MUSIC SALES LIMITED
Distribution Centre, Newmarket Road, Bury St Edmunds, Suffolk IP33 3YB, UK.
MUSIC SALES CORPORATION
257 Park Avenue South, New York, NY 10010, USA.
MUSIC SALES PTY LIMITED
20 Resolution Drive, Caringbah, NSW 2229, Australia.

Order No. CH76901
ISBN: 978-1-84938-562-6

Music by Howard Blake © 1982 by Highbridge Music Ltd.
This edition first published in 1986 by Highbridge Music Ltd/Faber Music Ltd.
Cover illustration by Raymond Briggs reproduced by permission of Snowman Enterprises Ltd.
All rights assigned to Chester Music Ltd, © 2010.
This edition engraved by Paul Ewers Music Design.
www.chesternovello.com

The Snowman is recorded complete on Sony 71116.
The piano score of *The Snowman* is available separately: CH76879.
The sheet music of *Walking in the Air* is available separately: CH77110.

Music by
Howard Blake

The Snowman

HOWARD BLAKE

1. Music-Box Dance

Tempo di valse

2. Walking In The Air

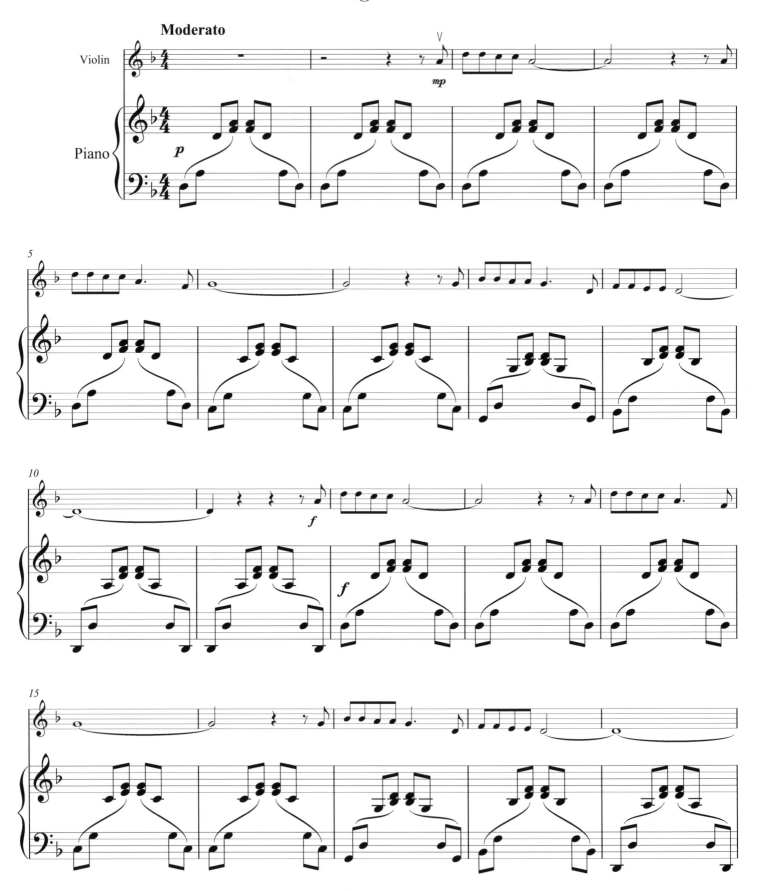

3. Dance Of The Snowmen